UNLEASHED

Releasing Power and Purpose in Your Work

TABLE OF CONTENTS

SMALL GROUP GUIDELINES

When new people join your group, review these guidelines for participating in a small group. These guidelines are intended to help create an environment where everyone feels safe to participate and share openly.

Safe Zone: Allow space for people to be heard and accepted.

Confidentiality: Whatever is shared during the group should not be shared outside of group with anyone unless it is your story, or you have received permission from the person who shared it.

Respect: When someone is giving their view or testimony, please do not interrupt. Allow them to complete their thought before asking questions or sharing your view.

Give your story, not advice: When someone shares do not respond with advice unless they specifically ask for it. If you begin a sentence with "you should" then it's advice.

Share your story: We all grow by hearing from each other. God brought you through your struggles to help someone else through theirs.

Allow time for others: We want to hear your story, but allow time for others to share as well.

HOW TO USE YOUR STUDY GUIDE

Each week, your group facilitator will take you through a series of scriptures related to a relevant work topic. Your study guide is divided into several sections to help facilitate your discussion.

Opening Discussion: We will begin each week with a question related to the topic for the week to help focus our attention and open the dialogue for all to participate.

Scripture: Take turns reading aloud our related scriptures for the week.

Group Discussion: Spend some time reviewing questions and discussing thoughts about the scripture.

Challenge for the Week: In order to allow the Holy Spirit to really make a lasting impact in our lives, we have to challenge ourselves to act on what we learn over the course of the week. Select a buddy from your group to help encourage one another and hold each other accountable.

Memory Verse: Each week we will have a key scripture to hold onto and memorize. Post this up in your office, on your bathroom mirror, on the refrigerator, or any other location you will see every day.

Closing Prayer: We will end in prayer, thanking God for his presence during the study and lifting up anyone in the group who is in need of prayer.

UNLEASHED

SESSION 1

INTRODUCTION

Opening Discussion:

Often times, we compartmentalize our lives between work, home, family, friends, etc. We might take on different roles in each of these environments depending on our personal responsibilities, expectations or social norms. We might believe this is a healthy approach because it creates boundaries or work-life balance. However, there is one aspect of our lives that is not intended to be limited to a single space, and that is our faith. The Holy Spirit is inside of us. It is with us every place we go, not just at church on Sunday. When we keep our faith separate from our work-life, we put limits on what is possible in our work and diminish the purpose we can find in it.

Is your relationship with God confined to morning devotion or church? How open are you to inviting Him into your daily work? What would it look like to do this?

_____

_____

Do you think integrating your faith into your work would bring you an advantage or disadvantage? What are some examples of both?

_____

_____

One of the incredible advantages of integrating your faith and work life is the unleashing of the power within us to transform our every thought, feeling and action. Over the course of this study, we are going to work together to allow God to transform the way we think about our work. As we change the way we think, it will change how we feel. When our feelings change, our attitude shifts and our behavior begins to align with the Spirit within us. This opens up space for God's Kingdom to come, and His will to be done here as in heaven.

As we begin, let's consider what it means for something to be unleashed. If you have ever had a dog, you have probably used a leash. There is a snap hook on the end of a line that connects to a ring on the collar of the dog. To unleash it, you have to open up the hook and release the collar. Similarly, for us to unleash the power and purpose of God in our work, we have to open ourselves as well.

What might a posture of openness look like for us? What do you need to release?

_____

_____

David demonstrated his spiritual openness by physically stretching out His hands to God, submitting that he needed Him the way dry land needs water.

> *I stretch out my hands to you; my soul thirsts for you like a parched land.*
>
> Psalm 143:6

With this same posture, our hands open to receive, let's listen to Paul's prayer to the Ephesians:

> *I pray that your hearts will be flooded with light so that you can* **understand the confident hope** *he has given to those he called—his holy people who are his rich and glorious inheritance. I also pray that you will* **understand the incredible greatness of God's power** *for us who believe him.*
>
> Ephesians 1:18-19

Group Discussion:
Paul prays for hearts to be "flooded with light so that" what can happen?

_____

_____

Notice he doesn't pray they receive confident hope and incredible power. Why? Because they already possess it. Instead he prays for light to illuminate their hearts so they understand what is already there. We typically think of understanding as something that comes from our mind. It is important to note Paul is praying for understanding in our heart. This is a deeper level of understanding from which we can fully utilize the incredible power inside.

Until you understand the incredible power you bring, it will lie dormant inside, just waiting for you to release it.

Challenge for the week:
This week's challenge is to spend some time thinking about the space you create in your work day for God to be present. Are you open to inviting God to join you in your work?

_____

_____

Spend some quiet time with God asking Him to help you understand the greatness you bring into your day and how you might unleash it.

Create a reminder that will prompt you during your day to acknowledge He is with you.

Prayer Requests:

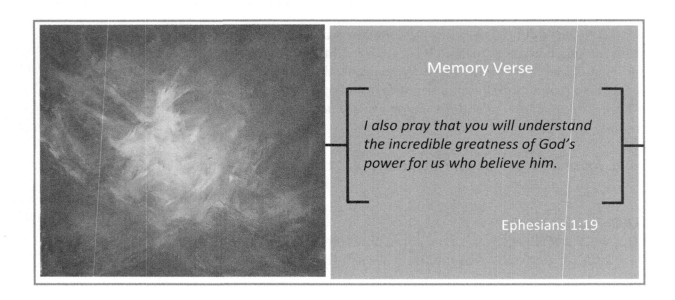

Memory Verse

I also pray that you will understand the incredible greatness of God's power for us who believe him.

Ephesians 1:19

UNLEASHED

SESSION 2

THE CHOICE

Opening Discussion:
During our first session, we discussed the importance of understanding the incredible power we have inside as believers. We challenged each other to consider how we might become more aware of it during our workday.

How have you found ways to create space for God in your work? If you haven't, what do you think has held you back?

_____

_____

Here is the interesting thing about having this incredible power in our lives: Even when we begin to understand it, we have to choose to unleash it. Today we are going to explore this choice, and how saying "yes" unleashes God's power in our lives.

> [1] *One day as Jesus was standing by the Lake of Gennesaret, the people were crowding around him and listening to the word of God.* [2] *He saw at the water's edge two boats, left there by the fishermen, who were washing their nets.* [3] *He got into one of the boats, the one belonging to Simon, and asked him to put out a little from shore. Then he sat down and taught the people from the boat.*
>
> [4] *When he had finished speaking, he said to Simon, "Put out into deep water, and let down the nets for a catch."*
>
> [5] *Simon answered, "Master, we've worked hard all night and haven't caught anything. But because you say so, I will let down the nets."*
>
> [6] *When they had done so, they caught such a large number of fish that their nets began to break.* [7] *So they signaled their partners in the other boat to come and help them, and they came and filled both boats so full that they began to sink.*
>
> Luke 5:1-7

Group Discussion:
Simon and the disciples witnessed a miracle. They saw the power of Jesus unleashed in their work. They were fisherman trying to catch fish. When Jesus said to put the nets back out,

Simon questioned him because of their lack of success all night. Yet through his choice to obey, the power of Jesus was unleashed, and they caught more than the boat could hold.

Do you believe God cares about the success of your work? Why or why not?

_____

_____

Jesus asked Simon to put the net out in deep water, something different from the way he thought it should be done. Simon's job was knowing how to catch fish, yet he submitted to Jesus in obedience. When you feel like the Holy Spirit is prompting you to do something, how do you respond? Do you question it against your own wisdom? Obey quickly? Delay obedience? Or dismiss it altogether? Share an example with your group.

_____

_____

Even after we witness the incredible greatness of God's power, we don't always make the choice to invite Him into our work-life. What are some reasons why we might not make this choice?

_____

_____

After witnessing the power of Jesus in his work, wouldn't you think Simon would want to take Him along on every expedition? Let's turn back to the Book of Luke and see how he responded:

> [8] When Simon Peter saw this, he fell at Jesus' knees and said, "Go away from me, Lord; I am a sinful man!" [9] For he and all his companions were astonished at the catch of fish they had taken, [10] and so were James and John, the sons of Zebedee, Simon's partners.
>
> Then Jesus said to Simon, "Don't be afraid; from now on you will fish for people." [11] So they pulled their boats up on shore, left everything and followed him.
>
> Luke 5:8-11

Group Discussion:
What are your thoughts about Simon Peter's response to witnessing the power of Jesus in his work? How can you relate to how he felt?

_____

_____

Jesus responds with "don't be afraid." Could it be fear that is holding you back from inviting God into your work? Are you ever afraid of what God might ask you to do if you open your work to Him?

_____

_____

If we can learn to trust that God wants a fulfilling life for us, what He dreamt for us before we were born, then perhaps we can begin to release our control over to Him and unleash confident hope and incredible power in our work. The choice is yours.

Challenge for the week:
This week's challenge is to look for ways to invite God into your work. Choose to say yes to any prompting you have from the Holy Spirit to act. Write about your experience below.

_____

_____

Prayer Requests:

Memory Verse

Simon answered, "Master, we've worked hard all night and haven't caught anything. But because you say so, I will let down the nets."

Luke 5:5

UNLEASHED

SESSION 3

KINGDOM PERSPECTIVE

Opening Discussion:

We talked in our first session about creating space to allow our minds to center on God's presence within our work. Last session we saw from Peter's example that miracles can happen when we obey in spite of what we think we know. Unleashing the power of God in our work, enables us to think about people, process and success differently than the way the world sees them. Throughout our time together, we are going to call this looking at our work from a Kingdom perspective.

Kingdom perspective requires us to shift our thinking, thought patterns and what is filling our minds from the world's viewpoint to God's viewpoint. It can be extremely difficult because we are surrounded by the allure of personal and financial success, titles and independence. This is the vantage point from which most people think and make decisions about their lives.

How do you think about your work, the company and your co-workers? Are you generally able to maintain a positive attitude throughout the day? If not, why?

_____

_____

When something goes wrong, do you typically focus on the positive or negative of the situation? Why do you think you respond one way or the other?

_____

_____

How we feel about our day is often determined by what happens around us, whether good or bad. If we unleash the power of the Holy Spirit into our work, we can learn to transform our thoughts in order to maintain a better overall mindset throughout our day.

> *Do not be conformed to this world, but be transformed by the **renewal of your mind**, that by testing you may discern what is the will of God, what is good and acceptable and perfect.*
>
> Romans 12:2

> *You were taught, with regard to your former way of life, to put off your old self, which is being corrupted by its deceitful desires; to be **made new in the attitude of your minds**; and to put on the new self, created to be like God in true righteousness and holiness.*
>
> Ephesians 4:22-24

Group Discussion:
How do we know what the will of God is?

_____

_____

Sometimes it is helpful to use scripture to understand God's will and His Kingdom perspective.

> And now, dear brothers and sisters, one final thing. **Fix your thoughts** on what is **true**, and **honorable**, and **right**, and **pure**, and **lovely**, and **admirable**. Think about things that are **excellent** and **worthy of praise**. Keep putting into practice all you learned and received from me— everything you heard from me and saw me doing. Then the God of peace will be with you.
>
> Philippians 4:8–9

Fix your thoughts...did you catch that? Most versions of the Bible say "think about these things."

This version of scripture speaks to the emphasis on "fix." It is a much stronger word than just thinking about something. Fixing your thoughts has an unwavering action to it. It not only securely holds God's truth in our minds, but it mends or repairs the worldly or negative thoughts that try and take up space there.

If we set our minds on bringing God's will into the moments of our lives, we will begin to see situations from His viewpoint, or a Kingdom perspective. When our thoughts do not line up, we can learn to take them captive and fix them.

> We demolish arguments and every pretension that sets itself up against the knowledge of God, and we **take captive every thought** to make it obedient to Christ.
>
> 2 Corinthians 10:5

Group discussion:
How do you take a thought captive and make it obedient to Christ?

_____

_____

Personal Exercise:
Paul says if we put this into practice, we will have peace. Let's give it a try right now. Think about a situation that happened this week that upset you.

_____

_____

Once you have the thought, go through these steps:

1. Review your experience in light of our scripture. Place a "✓" next to each one that aligns with your thought:

    ☐   It is **true.**
    ☐   It **honors** the other person.
    ☐   It is **right** and just.
    ☐   My motivation is **pure.**
    ☐   It is **lovely.**
    ☐   It is **admirable.**
    ☐   Is it **excellent.**
    ☐   It is **worthy of praise.** You would be proud to share it.

2. If your thought does not make it through the filter, then take it captive and fix it.

3. What is something positive about the person or situation? What good can come from it? Can you look at it from a different perspective and understand it better? What about it or the person is excellent and worthy of praise?

_____

_____

4. Think about those things.

Based on this exercise, how would a renewed mind offer an advantage to you in your work?

_____

_____

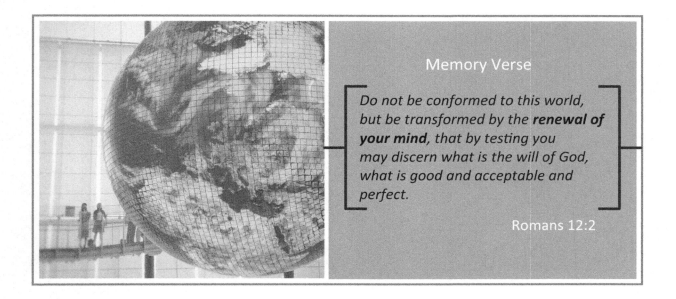

Memory Verse

*Do not be conformed to this world, but be transformed by the **renewal of your mind**, that by testing you may discern what is the will of God, what is good and acceptable and perfect.*

Romans 12:2

Challenge for the week:
This week's challenge is to begin to be aware of your thoughts in the moments of your day. Be mindful of the perspective from which you are thinking. When you find yourself thinking things that don't line up with God's heart or the Kingdom perspective, consider how you would change your thoughts so they line up. Use your checklist to guide you until it becomes a habit.

Prayer Requests:

UNLEASHED

SESSION 4

PURPOSE FOR WORK

Opening Discussion:

We have been discussing practicing mindfulness throughout our day to help us transform our thoughts about situations that arise, but what is your overall attitude about work? Is it something you have to do in order to provide for yourself and your family? Does it feel like meaningless toil? Or is it life-giving?

> *For a person may labor with wisdom, knowledge and skill, and then they must leave all they own to another who has not toiled for it. This too is meaningless and a great misfortune. What do people get for all the toil and anxious striving with which they labor under the sun? All their days their work is grief and pain; even at night their minds do not rest. This too is meaningless.*
>
> Ecclesiastes 2:21-23

How do you feel about your work? Do you agree with King Solomon's assessment? Or does it bring you satisfaction, fulfillment and purpose?

_____

_____

Interestingly, no matter how we feel about our current job, we would likely still work no matter how financially secure we were because we were created to work.

Working was part of our design BEFORE the fall. Original sin entered into the world and work then became toil. However, because of Jesus, we have not only been restored with God for eternity but also for the here and now.

Our work was included in this restoration.

If this is true, what does it mean for us today? How do we access the fullness of how work was designed to be for us? What is the purpose of it?

> *The LORD God took the man and put him in the Garden of Eden to **work (avodah)** it and take care of it.*
>
> Genesis 2:15

The Hebrew word "avodah" used here means work, worship, and service.

The world's view of work is only focused on what you do for a living. It is your position, title and how you make money. It's no wonder it feels like meaningless toil or a curse that produces thorns and thistles. The Kingdom perspective on work is so much more. God's view of our work combines what we do with worship and service. The unity of all three unleashes purpose in our work-life.

Group Discussion:
How would your view of work change if you looked at it in light of this concept? Is this possible?

_____

_____

Does it matter what career we choose? In other words is **what** we do for our job important? Why or why not?

_____

_____

What we do should never define who we are. However, the work we do is certainly a reflection of how we were designed and who created us.

> There are different kinds of working, but in all of them and in everyone it
> is the same God at work.
>
> 1 Corinthians 12:6

The position we hold might be very different, but what we have in common is that each of us are designed with certain gifts, strengths and abilities that are a direct reflection of our creator. Did you know that you were given specific strengths and abilities to help you do work while you are here? You might think something that just comes natural to you is something everyone can do. However, that often is not the case. It is likely a gift that was given to you for a specific assignment for the Kingdom.

> *For we are his workmanship, created in Christ Jesus for **good works**, which God prepared beforehand, that we should walk in them.*
>
> Ephesians 2:10

> *For as in one body we have many members, and the members do not all have the same function, so we, though many, are one body in Christ, and individually members one of another. Having **gifts that differ** according to the grace given to us, let us use them: if prophecy, in proportion to our faith; if service, in our serving; the one who teaches, in his teaching; the one who exhorts, in his exhortation; the one who contributes, in generosity; the one who leads, with zeal; the one who does acts of mercy, with cheerfulness.*
>
> Romans 12:4-8

Group Discussion:
How do these scripture help us understand the importance of what we do for our work?

_____

_____

Take a moment and share some of the gifts/talents you have. How are they contributing to your work? Are any of them not being exercised?

_____

_____

What we do is important because it is how we utilize the gifts and talents we have been given. It doesn't have to be a direct aspect of our paying job, but it is part of our life's work (purpose) while we are here on Earth.

Challenge for the week:
Perhaps you are not sure what talents you have been given. Spend some time this week in discovery.

1. Ask some friends and co-workers what strengths they see in you.

_____

_____

Memory Verse

*For we are his workmanship, created in Christ Jesus for **good works**, which God prepared beforehand, that we should walk in them.*

Ephesians 2:10

2. Take the FREE personal strengths assessment @ www.high5test.com. Capture your results here:

_____

_____

_____

_____

Set aside 15-20 minutes to talk with God about how your strengths line up with what you do. Ask Him to show your other ways you can utilize your strengths to build the Kingdom.

Be prepared to share one of your top 5 with your group next session.

Prayer Requests:

UNLEASHED

SESSION 5

WORK IS WORSHIP

Opening Discussion:
What is one of your top 5 strengths from the assessment? How is it utilized in what you do currently?

_____

_____

If you recall from our last session, Avodah, God's view of work, is the unity of work, worship and service. What we do is not the singular purpose for work. Our work is also intended to be worship.

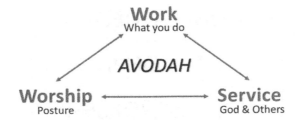

What is worship? Why do we do it? How do you express it?

_____

_____

> Therefore let us be **grateful for receiving a kingdom that cannot be shaken**, and thus let us offer to God acceptable **worship**, with reverence and awe, for our God is a consuming fire.
>
> Hebrews 12:28-29

> And so, dear brothers and sisters, I plead with you to give your bodies to God **because of all he has done for you**. Let them be a living and holy sacrifice—the kind he will find acceptable. This is truly the way to **worship** him.
>
> Romans 12:1

Group Discussion:
We worship out of our gratitude for what God has done in our lives, but do you do this in your work? How can your work be an act of worship?

_____

_____

Everything we do can be an act of worship if our posture is towards God. Today we are going to discuss three simple ways we can incorporate worship into our daily work.

> **Rejoice** *always,* **pray** *continually,* **give thanks** *in all circumstances; for this is God's will for you in Christ Jesus.*
>
> 1 Thessalonians 5:16-18

REJOICE ALWAYS

> **Always be full of joy** *in the Lord. I say it again—rejoice!*
>
> Philippians 4:4

> *Work with* **enthusiasm,** *as though you were working for the Lord rather than for people.*
>
> Ephesians 6:7

How can you incorporate a posture of **rejoicing** in your work?

_____

_____

PRAY CONTINUALLY

> *I urge you, first of all, to* **pray** *for all people. Ask God to help them; intercede on their behalf, and give thanks for them.* **Pray** *this way for kings and all who are in authority so that we can live peaceful and quiet lives marked by godliness and dignity. This is good and pleases God our Savior, who wants everyone to be saved and to understand the truth.*
>
> 1 Timothy 1:1-4

> *Don't worry about anything; instead,* **pray about everything.** *Tell God what you need, and thank him for all he has done.*
>
> Philippians 4:6

How can you incorporate a posture of **praying** continually into your work?

_____

_____

GIVE THANKS

*Let the message about Christ, in all its richness, fill your lives. Teach and counsel each other with all the wisdom he gives. Sing psalms and hymns and spiritual songs to God with **thankful hearts**. And whatever you do or say, do it as a **representative of the Lord Jesus, giving thanks** through him to God the Father.*

Colossians 3:16-17

*I will **give thanks** to you, LORD, with all my heart; I will tell of all your wonderful deeds.*

Psalm 9:1

What would it look like for you to **give thanks** in all circumstances at work?

_____

_____

Just as praise and worship are lifted up both in good times and when life hits us hard, so it is with our work. We rejoice, pray and give thanks to God for our work both when it is going well and when we need to take on a second job to pay rent and keep food on the table. Letting go of the worry and fear creates space for to God brings hope into all situations and move on our behalf.

Work as worship is about understanding that every task we do during our workday is intended to be done for God and with God.

Unleashing His power into our work, enables us to change the way we think about even the smallest, most dreaded task during our week. It takes on significant meaning and purpose because it is a loving, honoring response of thanksgiving and praise to our God.

Memory Verse

Rejoice always, **pray** continually, **give thanks** in all circumstances; for this is God's will

1 Thessalonians 5:16-18

Challenge for the week:

Spend some time each morning this week reviewing your calendar before you start your day.

Which meetings or tasks do you need to shift your thinking from work to worship?

_____

_____

How can you incorporate rejoicing, praying and giving thanks into your day?

_____

_____

Prayer Requests:

UNLEASHED

SESSION 6

SERVE GOD

Opening Discussion:

Over the last few sessions, we have been talking about how our work is so much more than what we do. How it can also be an act of worship when we offer it in response to God through rejoicing, praying and giving thanks. The work we do has been prepared in advance for us and flows from our worship by using the gifts we have been given.

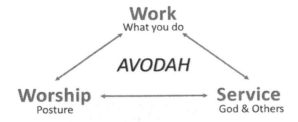

What about service? Are you in the service industry? Who do you serve in your work?

_____

_____

Everything we do serves someone. Unfortunately that can be ourselves if we are not living a fully integrated life.

> *No one can serve two masters. Either you will hate the one and love the other, or you will be devoted to the one and despise the other. You cannot serve both God and money.*
>
> Matthew 6:24

While our work is a means for us to make money, it should not be the purpose for our work. From the Kingdom perspective, it serves a greater purpose. It is intended to be service to God and others.

Serve God. Serve others.

Over the next two sessions, we are going to unpack what it looks like to serve God and others through our work. Today we are going to focus on how our work is service to God.

Group Discussion:

Do we have to be a missionary or work at a church or non-profit to serve God in our work?

SESSION 6— SERVE GOD

What are some ways we can serve God through our work?

_____

_____

Does serving God feel like a duty or a gift to honor him?

_____

_____

Paul's message on how we should work does not focus on what we do for a living, but how we do our work and who we are serving.

> *Never be lazy, but work hard and serve the Lord enthusiastically.*
>
> Romans 12:11 (NLT)

> *Therefore, my dear brothers and sisters, stand firm. Let nothing move you. Always give yourselves fully to the work of the Lord, because you know that your labor in the Lord is not in vain.*
>
> 1 Corinthians 15:58

> *Do all things without grumbling or disputing; so that you will prove yourselves to be blameless and innocent, children of God above reproach in the midst of a crooked and perverse generation, among whom you appear as lights in the world, holding fast the word of life, so that in the day of Christ I will have reason to glory because I did not run in vain nor toil in vain.*
>
> Philippians 2:14-16

Work is not toil when it focuses on serving God. It becomes an opportunity to show our faith and be a light in the world.

Do you believe that the way you approach your work (not words spoken) could actually show people your faith and love for God? How is that possible?

_____

_____

Let's review and discuss how today's scriptures can teach us practical ways we can serve God through our actions at work:

- Work hard (Romans 12:11)
- Work with enthusiasm (Romans 12:11)
- Let nothing move you (1 Corinthians 15:58) – don't compromise your values
- Always give yourself fully (1 Corinthians 15:58) – be engaged and focused
- Without grumbling or disputing (Philippians 2:14) – keep a positive attitude

Which of the above is an area of strength for you at work?

_____

_____

What would it take for you to put these ideas into practice?

_____

_____

We can serve God through mission work, helping the homeless or other philanthropic ways, but if we close Him out of our work, we are missing a significant part of our daily lives. He created us to work. Why not glorify Him by serving Him daily through how we go about our work? Your work pleases God. Let it be a reflection of your faith.

Challenge for the week:
Review the ways your work can be service to God. Look at the tasks you do this week as an opportunity to display your faith and your love for God.

Prayer Requests:

Memory Verse

Never be lazy, but work hard and serve the Lord enthusiastically.

Romans 12:11 (NLT)

UNLEASHED

SESSION 7

SERVE OTHERS

Opening Discussion:

Last session we talked about our work being an opportunity to serve God and show our love for Him. When we serve God our work is worship, the same love God has for us overflows, spilling out to those around us.

Work is an opportunity to express God's love to others through serving them.

Practically every type of work involves some interaction with others. Even if we work alone, we have to sell our product or service to others. These interactions provide an opportunity for us to express God's love. Again, it doesn't matter what role or position you have. God has given all of us the same authority and responsibility as it relates to sharing His love. It's how people will know that we are His disciples.

> *"I give you a new command: Love one another. Just as I have loved you, you must also love one another. By this all people will know that you are My disciples, if you have love for one another."*
>
> John 13:34-35

Every encounter with someone at work is an opportunity to express God's love for that person by serving them. We can do this by putting other's interests above our own:

> *Therefore if you have any encouragement from being united with Christ, if any comfort from his love, if any common sharing in the Spirit, if any tenderness and compassion, then make my joy complete by being like-minded,* **having the same love**, *being one in spirit and of one mind. Do nothing out of selfish ambition or vain conceit. Rather, in humility value others above yourselves, not looking to your own interests but each of you to the interests of the others.*
>
> Philippians 2:1-4

We serve others through our work by allowing the same spirit we have offered to God in our worship to be unleashed to all those around us. We can demonstrate God's love in our relationships, through showing compassion, love and respect for each person we encounter.

COMPASSION

Where there is compassion, there is passion to serve.

*In everything I did, I showed you that by this kind of hard work we must **help the weak**, remembering the words the Lord Jesus himself said: "It is more blessed to give than to receive."*

Acts 20:35

Group discussion:

What breaks your heart? Those are the areas where you will feel the most purpose in serving. Who are you helping?

_____

_____

LOVE

Love excludes no one.

If someone says, "I love God," but hates a fellow believer, that person is a liar; for if we don't love people we can see, how can we love God, whom we cannot see? And he has given us this command: Those who love God must also love their fellow believers.

1 John 4:20-21

What does it mean to love our co-workers? How do we do it? We can find some great advice in an unexpected scripture that we so often hear at weddings. Think about your co-workers as you listen.

Love is patient, love is kind. It does not envy, it does not boast, it is not proud. It does not dishonor others, it is not self-seeking, it is not easily angered, it keeps no record of wrongs. Love does not delight in evil but rejoices with the truth. It always protects, always trusts, always hopes, always perseveres.

1 Corinthians 13:4-7

Group Discussion:

How well do you love those around you at work? What are some ways this scripture helps us show our love for others?

_____

_____

What part of the scripture do you find difficult to do at work?

_____

_____

RESPECT

Honor leadership.

> *Dear brothers and sisters, **honor** those who are your leaders in the Lord's work. They work hard among you and give you spiritual guidance. Show them great **respect** and wholehearted love because of their work. And live peacefully with each other.*
>
> 1 Thessalonians 5:12-13

Group Discussion:
How do you show respect for leadership when you disagree with their decision or have conflicting personalities or moral standards?

_____

_____

What you do for work may or may not line up ideally with your gifts and talents, but it always creates a space for you to worship God and serve Him. It also provides opportunities to love and serve others. As you continue to find ways to unify work, worship and service, you will release your unique Kingdom purpose into your work.

Challenge for the week:
Show God's love through your actions. Be intentional to do one thing this week for someone while at work to let someone know that God loves them.

Prayer Requests:

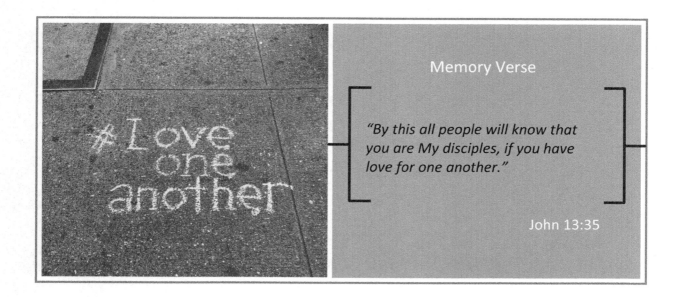

Memory Verse

"By this all people will know that you are My disciples, if you have love for one another."

John 13:35

UNLEASHED

SESSION 8

SETTING OUR AIM

Opening Discussion:
Take a minute and think about what the word "success" means to you? What are some words that come to mind?

_____

_____

Webster defines success as "the attainment of popularity or profit" or "a person or thing that achieves desired aims or attained prosperity."

What is your desired aim for your work? Why do you want to be successful?

_____

_____

In a dream the Lord told Solomon to ask for anything, and He would give it to him.

Here is what the young king asked:

> "Now, Lord my God, you have made your servant king in place of my father David. But I am only a little child and do not know how to carry out my duties. Your servant is here among the people you have chosen, a great people, too numerous to count or number. So give your servant a discerning heart to govern your people and to distinguish between right and wrong. For who is able to govern this great people of yours?"
>
> 1 Kings 3:6-9

Group Discussion:
What do you think King Solomon's desired aim for success was based on this scripture?

_____

_____

We find a humble, uncertain young king seeking wisdom and discernment in order to better serve God's people. Sounds a lot like our discussion the last few sessions about serving God and serving others. God was pleased with his selfless request, so He gave Solomon what he asked plus wealth and honor.

King Solomon reigned for 40 years. With his servant leader mindset and outward focused start, we might all agree he had set the right aim for success.

Let's take a look at the end of his reign to see how it went:

> *I undertook great projects: I built houses for myself and planted
> vineyards. I made gardens and parks and planted all kinds of fruit trees in
> them. I made reservoirs to water groves of flourishing trees. I bought
> male and female slaves and had other slaves who were born in my house.
> I also owned more herds and flocks than anyone in Jerusalem before me. I
> amassed silver and gold for myself, and the treasure of kings and
> provinces. I acquired male and female singers, and a harem as well—the
> delights of a man's heart. I became greater by far than anyone in
> Jerusalem before me. In all this my wisdom stayed with me.*
> > *I denied myself nothing my eyes desired;*
> > *I refused my heart no pleasure.*
> > *My heart took delight in all my labor,*
> > *and this was the reward for all my toil.*
>
> Ecclesiastes 2:4-10

Group Discussion:
Review the scripture above. Underline or circle every time Solomon refers to himself. How many instances did you find?

_____

_____

How does this differ from the young King Solomon we discussed earlier? What do you think caused this significant shift in focus from others to self?

_____

_____

Power, popularity, prosperity, wealth, women and wisdom, King Solomon was a living definition of worldly success, but did he achieve his desired aim for success we discussed earlier?

Here is how he summed up his life achievement:

Yet when I surveyed all that my hands had done
and what I had toiled to achieve,
everything was meaningless, a chasing after the wind;
nothing was gained under the sun.

Ecclesiastes 2:4-11

Group Discussion:
How have you related to Solomon's story? When do you find yourself struggling to stay focused on the Kingdom perspective of success?

_____

_____

Sometimes we, like Solomon, get caught up in worldly desires for success and forget we are part of a bigger story. You were given talents, but they aren't for your personal gain. Remember the money in the parable of the talents? That was the master's money which he entrusted to the servants while he was away. Our bigger story is that our Father has entrusted us with certain gifts and abilities that will bring His Kingdom to earth. We can choose to use them to build for Him or our own gain.

Do you not know that in a race all the runners run, but only one gets the
prize? Run in such a way as to get the prize. Everyone who competes in
the games goes into strict training. They do it to get a crown that will not
last, but we do it to get a crown that will last forever.

1 Corinthians 9:24-25

Where are you going to set your aim? Will it be on earthly treasure and the world's view of success? Or on a crown that will last forever?

Challenge for the week:
Spend some quiet time with God reflecting on your view of success. Consider journaling what lasting success looks like in your work. Where are you currently missing the mark and how might you redirect your aim?

Prayer Requests:

Memory Verse

Do you not know that in a race all the runners run, but only one gets the prize? Run in such a way as to get the prize.

1 Corinthians 9:24

UNLEASHED

SESSION 9

LASTING SUCCESS

Opening Discussion:
We ended our last session talking about setting our aim on a crown that lasts forever. What does that mean? What are some things that last forever?

_____

_____

If you recall King Solomon from our last discussion, he realized that although he had gained every possession under the sun, none of it mattered for none of it could be kept or enjoyed after he passed from this life. The work to gain it didn't count for anything upon leaving this world. He wrote:

> *Everyone comes naked from their mother's womb, and as everyone*
> *comes, so they depart. They take nothing from their toil that they can*
> *carry in their hands. This too is a grievous evil: As everyone comes, so they*
> *depart, and what do they gain, since they toil for the wind?*
>
> Ecclesiastes 5:15-16

Group Discussion:
The house, car, money, job, none of it can be taken with you. If this is true, what is the purpose of generating wealth while we are here?

_____

_____

A hint is found in the Book of Luke when Jesus tells the story of the dishonest manager. In the story, a manager was fired by the owner of a business. The fired manager went out and re-wrote the debts people owed the owner so the debt on the ledger approximately 50% of the true debt. He was using money to gain friends, so when he lost his job, there would be someone there for him. The business owner actually applauded the ex-manager for his shrewdness. Jesus used this story to teach a lesson about wealth:

> *Here's the lesson: Use your worldly resources to benefit others and make*
> *friends. Then, when your possessions are gone, they will welcome you to*
> *an eternal home.*
>
> Luke 16:9

King Solomon said we can't carry anything in our hands when we leave this world.. Jesus is saying use worldly wealth to help people so you gain friends and they welcome you into heaven. Could it be possible that the relationships we build here are what lasts forever?

> *"Do not store up for yourselves treasures on earth, where moths and vermin destroy, and where thieves break in and steal. But store up for yourselves **treasures in heaven**, where moths and vermin do not destroy, and where thieves do not break in and steal."*
>
> *Matthew 6:19-20*

Group Discussion:
Based on today's scriptures and our discussion, what do you think Jesus means by "treasures in heaven"?

_____

_____

How might the workplace be used for investing into Kingdom wealth? What things might you need to change to begin building into this eternal investment account?

_____

_____

Paul also speaks to how we can use our wealth to store up treasures in heaven:

> *Teach those who are rich in this world not to be proud and not to trust in their money, which is so unreliable. Their trust should be in God, who richly gives us all we need for our enjoyment. Tell them to use their money to do good. They should be rich in good works and generous to those in need, always being ready to share with others. By doing this they will be storing up their treasure as a good foundation for the future so that they may experience true life.*
>
> *1 Timothy 6:17-19 NLT*

How does he suggest we use our resources for lasting success?

_____

_____

It is important to note that none of these scriptures say that worldly wealth is bad. Actually, the more prosperous you are, the more you can help others. The caution against worldly wealth is to not rely on it as our source of security, happiness or become prideful in what you have. If our focus becomes solely on the money or earthly things, we will miss out on the joy it can bring us. Jesus spoke about this idea as well:

> And he went on to say to them all, "Watch out and guard yourselves from every kind of greed; because your **true life** is not made up of the things you own, no matter how rich you may be."
>
> Luke 12:15 ESV

Group Discussion:
What is "true life" and how do we experience it?

_____

_____

Are the things you are striving to gain in this world lasting or will they be forgotten?

_____

_____

Relationships are right in front of you on a daily basis. Opportunities to build into your eternal treasures. Set your aim on investing into them. It is how you can find purpose in your work and lasting success. As we continue on our journey, we will be diving into Kingdom relationships and how to further unleash God's power in them.

Challenge for the week:
Spend some quiet time with God reflecting on your view of relationships. How would you treat others differently if you knew you were building eternal friendships? Who is someone you can invest in over the next 6 months?

Prayer Requests:

Memory Verse

Here's the lesson: Use your worldly resources to benefit others and make friends. Then, when your possessions are gone, they will welcome you to an eternal home.

Luke 16:9